I am a Goddess
Colour your Way to Self-Love

Illustrated by Kat Shaw

Girl God Books

Copyright 2022
All Rights Reserved

ISBN 978-82-93725-28-2

Girl God Books are also available at discount for retail, wholesale, and bulk purchase.
For details, contact us at support@girlgod.org.

katshaw.art

Girl God Books

The Girl God
A book for children young and old, celebrating the Divine Female by Trista Hendren. Magically illustrated by Elisabeth Slettnes with quotes from various faith traditions and feminist thinkers.

Willendorf's Legacy: The Sacred Body
Travel through time and discover a world where the fullness of women was both admired and deified. Reclaim your beautiful Goddess body through the rich pages of this powerful collection of art, poetry and essays celebrating our divine inheritance as daughters of Willendorf.

Re-Membering with Goddess: Healing the Patriarchal Perpetuation of Trauma
Re-Membering with Goddess is an anthology of women's experiences of trauma—trauma as a result of patriarchy; trauma perpetuated by patriarchy; and how through personal healing of trauma the Goddess is re-membered, re-embodied and resurrected.

Just as I Am: Hymns Affirming the Divine Female
What is a Hermnal? It's the collective sigh of our ancestral Grandmothers. It's a means of drawing us closer together as Sisters. It is a compilation of songs that affirms our Sacredness, apart from Man, and assures us that we are Sovereign Beings and Creatrixes, too. And it is our Love Gift of Gratitude to Mama.

Re-visioning Medusa: from Monster to Divine Wisdom
A remarkable collection of essays, poems, and art by scholars who have researched Her, artists who have envisioned Her, and women who have known Her in their personal story. All have spoken with Her and share something of their communion in this anthology.

Original Resistance: Reclaiming Lilith, Reclaiming Ourselves
Through poetry, prose, incantation, prayer and imagery, women from all walks of life invite you to join them in the revolutionary act of claiming their place—of reclaiming themselves.

In Defiance of Oppression - The Legacy of Boudica
In Defiance of Oppression - The Legacy of Boudica is an anthology that encapsulates the Spirit of the defiant warrior in a modern apathetic age. No longer will the voices of our sisters go unheard, as the ancient Goddesses return to the battlements, calling to ignite the spark within each and every one of us—to defy oppression wherever we find it, and stand together in solidarity. Delve into the pages and remember the spirit of defiance within you. We are still here, we are standing with you, and we shall never, ever, give up.

Warrior Queen: Answering the Call of The Morrigan
Warrior Queen: Answering the Call of The Morrigan is a powerful anthology about the Irish Celtic Goddess. Each contributor brings The Morrigan to life with unique stories that invite readers to partake and inspire them to pen their own. Included are essays, poems, stories, chants, rituals, and art from dozens of story-tellers and artists from around the world, illustrating and recounting the many ways this powerful Goddess of war, death, and prophecy has changed their lives.

www.thegirlgod.com

Additional Offerings by Kat Shaw

Changing history to HERstory
Changing history to HERstory is based on the ground-breaking and uplifting art exhibition by Kat Shaw, highlighting the amazing women who have walked before us and changed the world.

Walking the Path of Kali
This book aims to lead you, through walking your own path, around the wheel of Kali throughout the year, and establishing a direct and individual connection with Her – whilst remembering that She is and always has been within us all

The Path of Kali Oracle
A set of 54 cards containing 18 archetype cards, 18 affirmation cards and 18 symbol cards along with 18 corresponding crystals to guide you, empower you, offer insights and impart wisdom into your soul from the very essence of Kali. This deck facilitates integration of Kali's teachings into your life by feeling, knowing and walking alongside Her 18 archetypes.

Volume 1&2: The Path of the Divine Feminine Empowering Goddess Oracle Cards
Each volume includes a set of 60 stunning oracle cards, painted and written with love. These glorious oracle decks will enable you to step into the incredible teachings, healing, wisdom and adoration of the Goddess in her many, many faces as She awakens your soul and brings magic and empowerment into your life.

Imperfectly Fabulous Empowering Affirmation Cards for the 21st Century Goddess
A set of 75 inspirational cards, painted and written with love. These cards will empower your soul as you rise and awaken your inner Goddess – stepping into the Divine Feminine who resides inside the glorious woman that you are – totally in your own skin, loving, powerful, strong and full of magic – embracing your fabulous imperfections and owning your magnificence exactly as you are meant to be.

And Still I Rise
A book based on the inspirational exhibition by Kat Shaw featuring 85 glorious women who have survived, and used the broken pieces of their lives to build a bridge and walk with power. Coming soon!

Prints, canvasses, cards, original paintings and merchandise are also available at the KatShawArtist Etsy shop: Www.Etsy.com/uk/shop/KatShawArtist

As always, this book is dedicated to my reason for breathing - my daughter. May you always know how powerful you are.

Let me introduce you to my colouring book.

I have been wanting to make one for quite some time, so I am delighted that it finds itself in your hands.

It was suggested that I should get technical and download the images into a design software package to make them colouring book-worthy. There are 2 reasons I didn't do this – 1) because I hate technology and would not have a clue how to do that 2) because, for me, the magic is in the creation of the image. Working in sacred space, with intention - painting the empowerment and the love and the healing and the absolute vibe into the Goddess. So, to simply make these Goddesses "just" a computer-generated image didn't resonate with my soul.

Instead, I sat for weeks and drew the glorious Goddesses again, honouring each and every magnificent curve, dip and undulation.

This is the reason you will see different thicknesses of lines and wobbly edges. Imperfections, flaws.

But this is life, right? It isn't perfect – it's real.

So, what you have here are drawings made in love and honour of the Divine Feminine and all of you. They show the flaws and the imperfections, but they are, and always will be beautiful – just like you.

As you colour these pages, listen to the words of the Goddess. Listen to their teachings, their wisdom. Hear them cheering you on. Feel their love. Allow their strength and fire to imbue into your soul. Laugh with them and cry with them, but most importantly, colour your way to self-love.

Love,

Kat

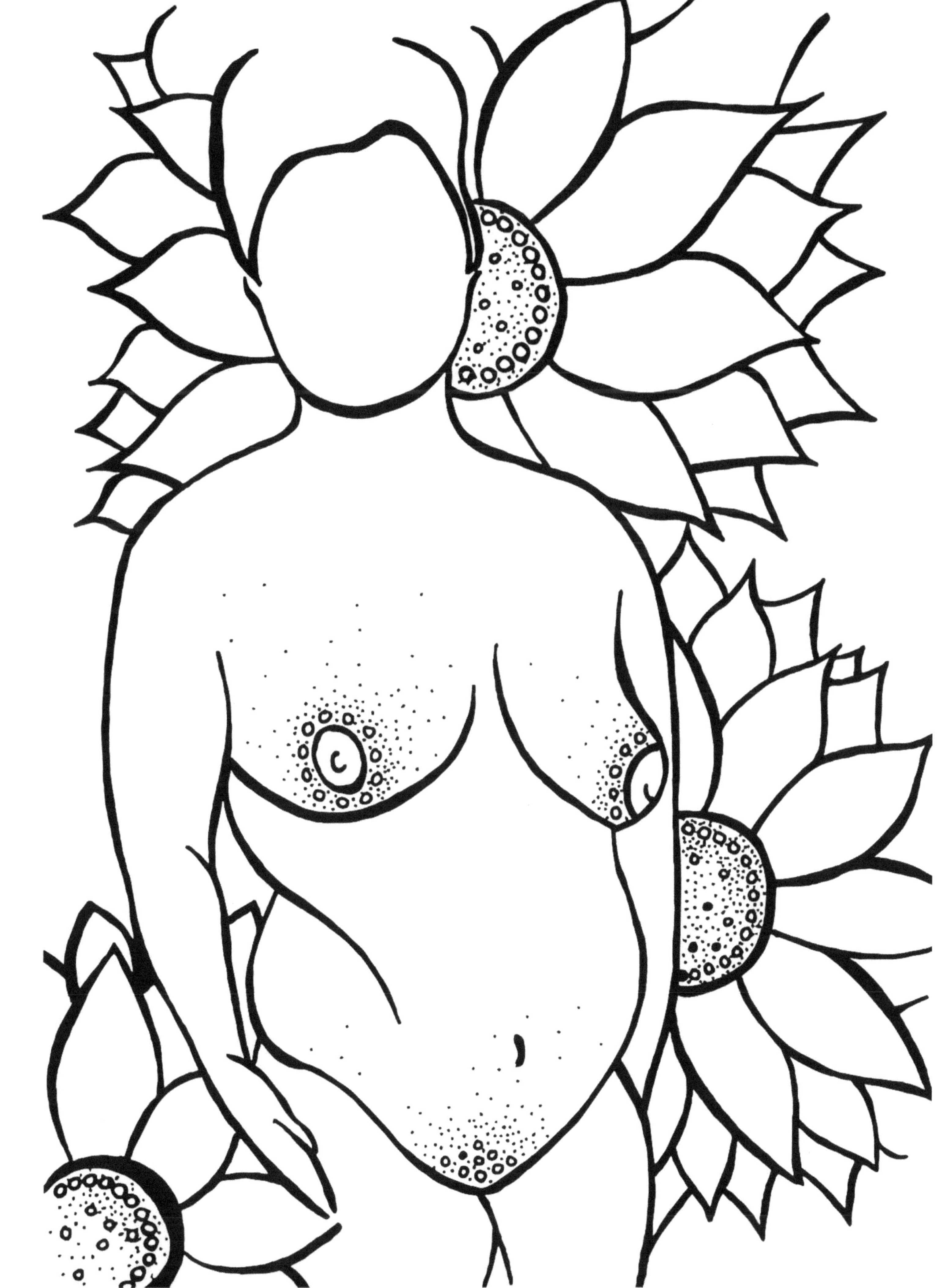

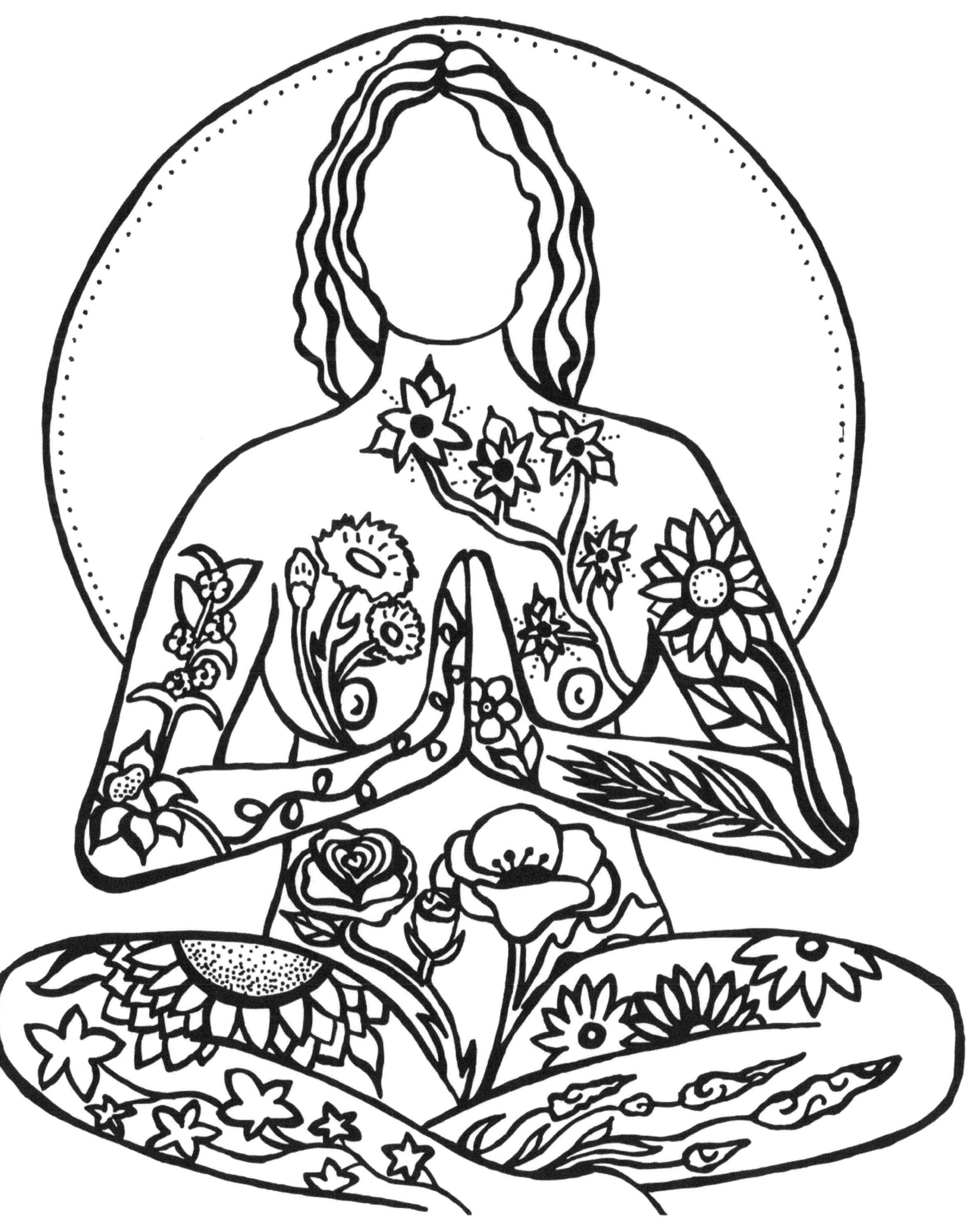

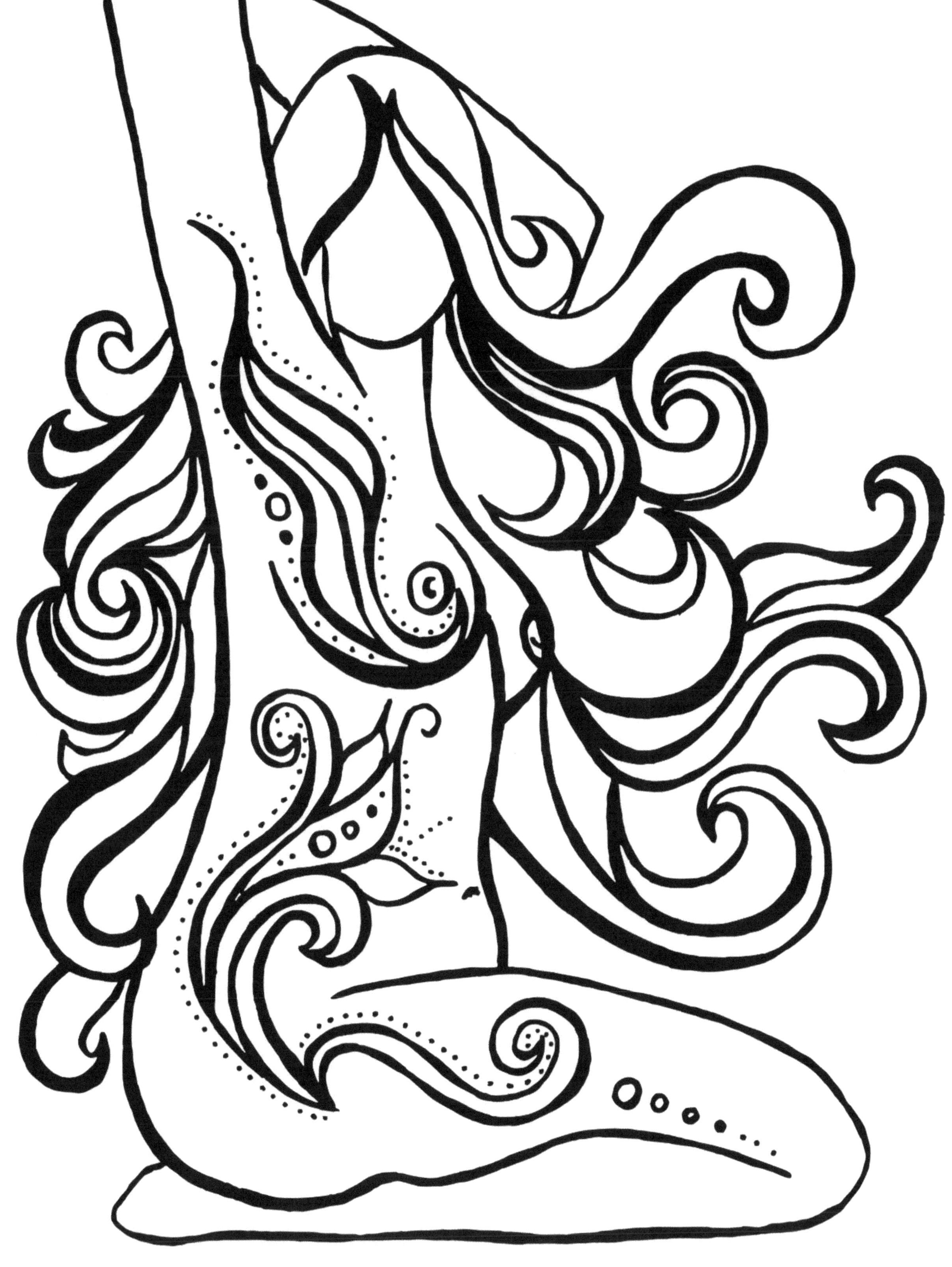

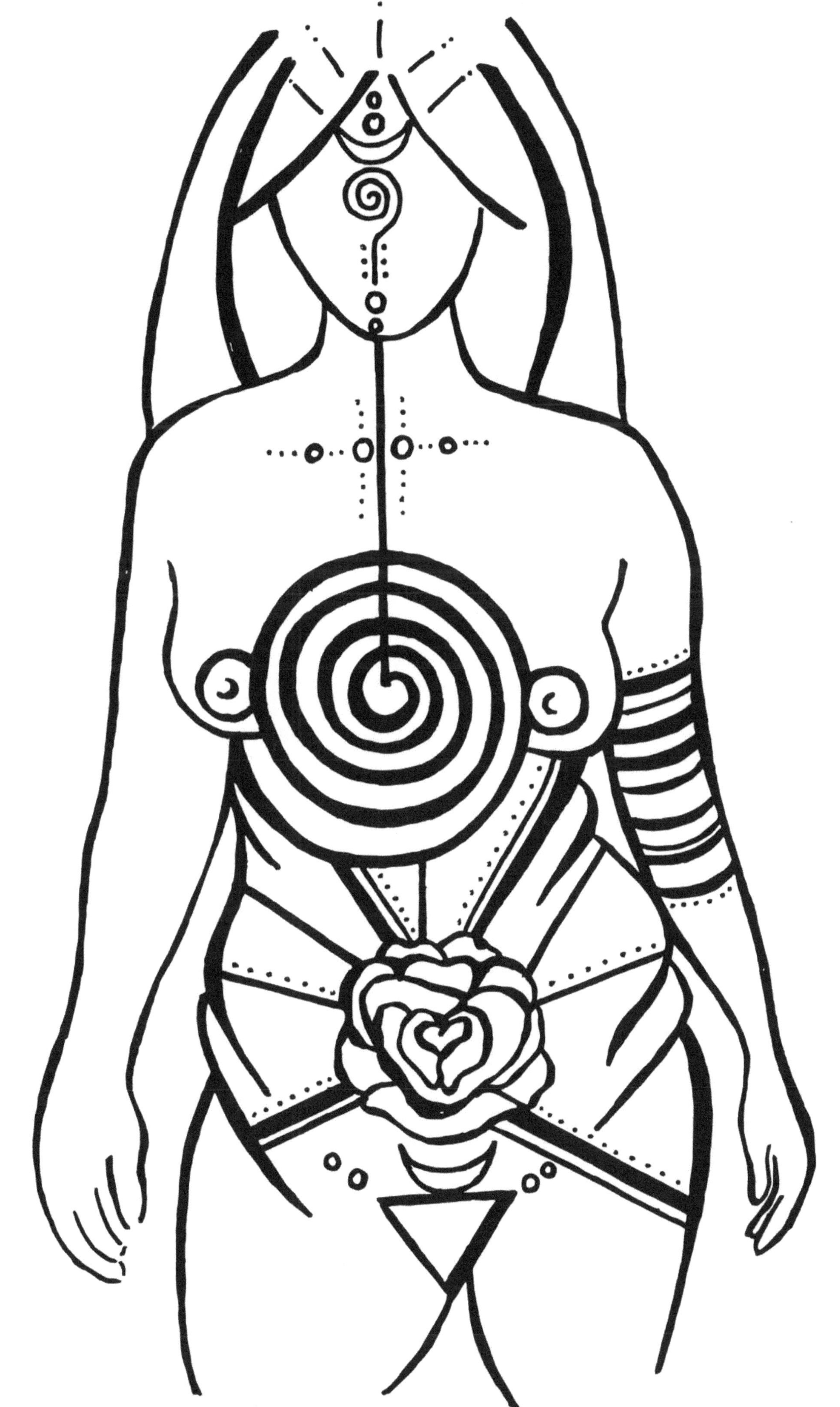

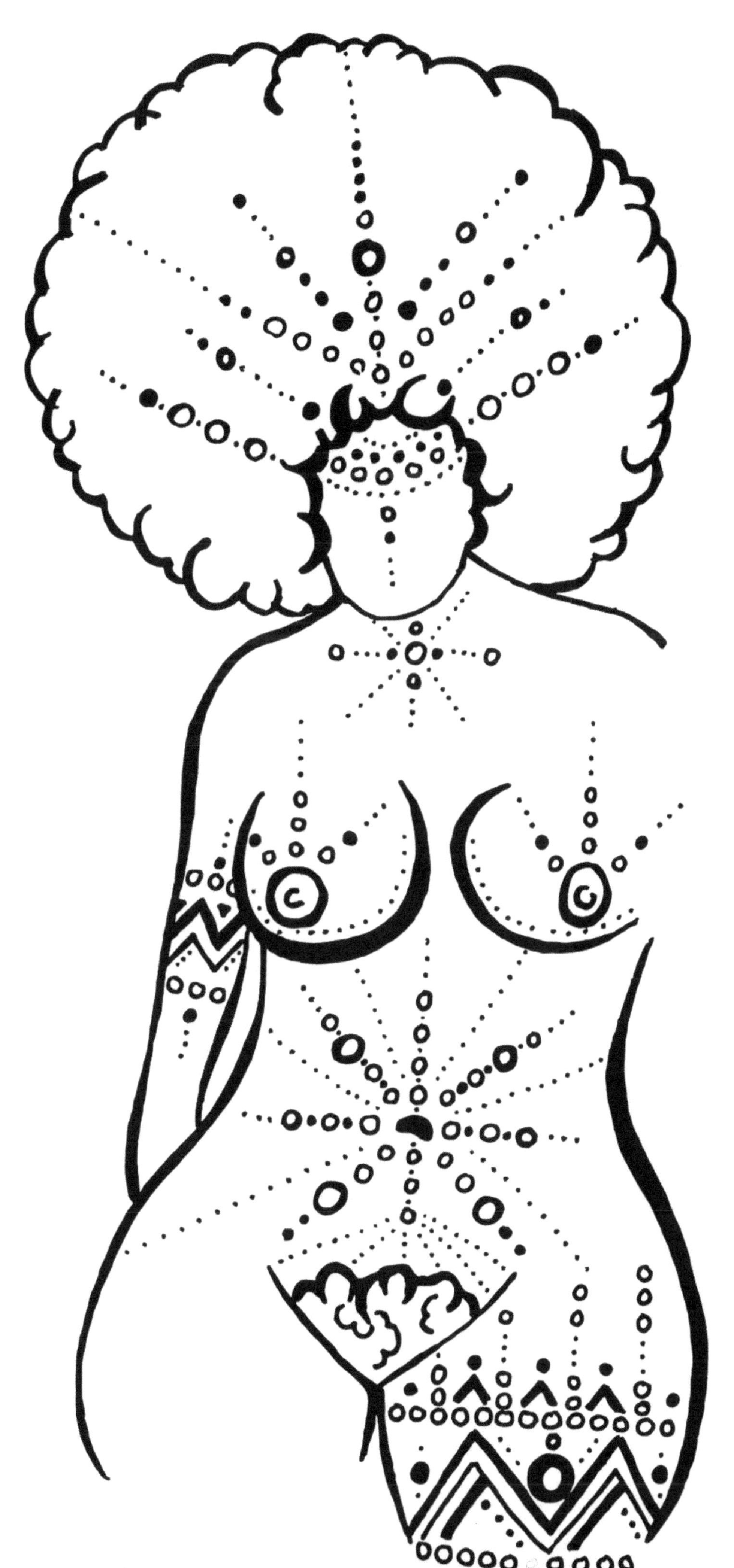

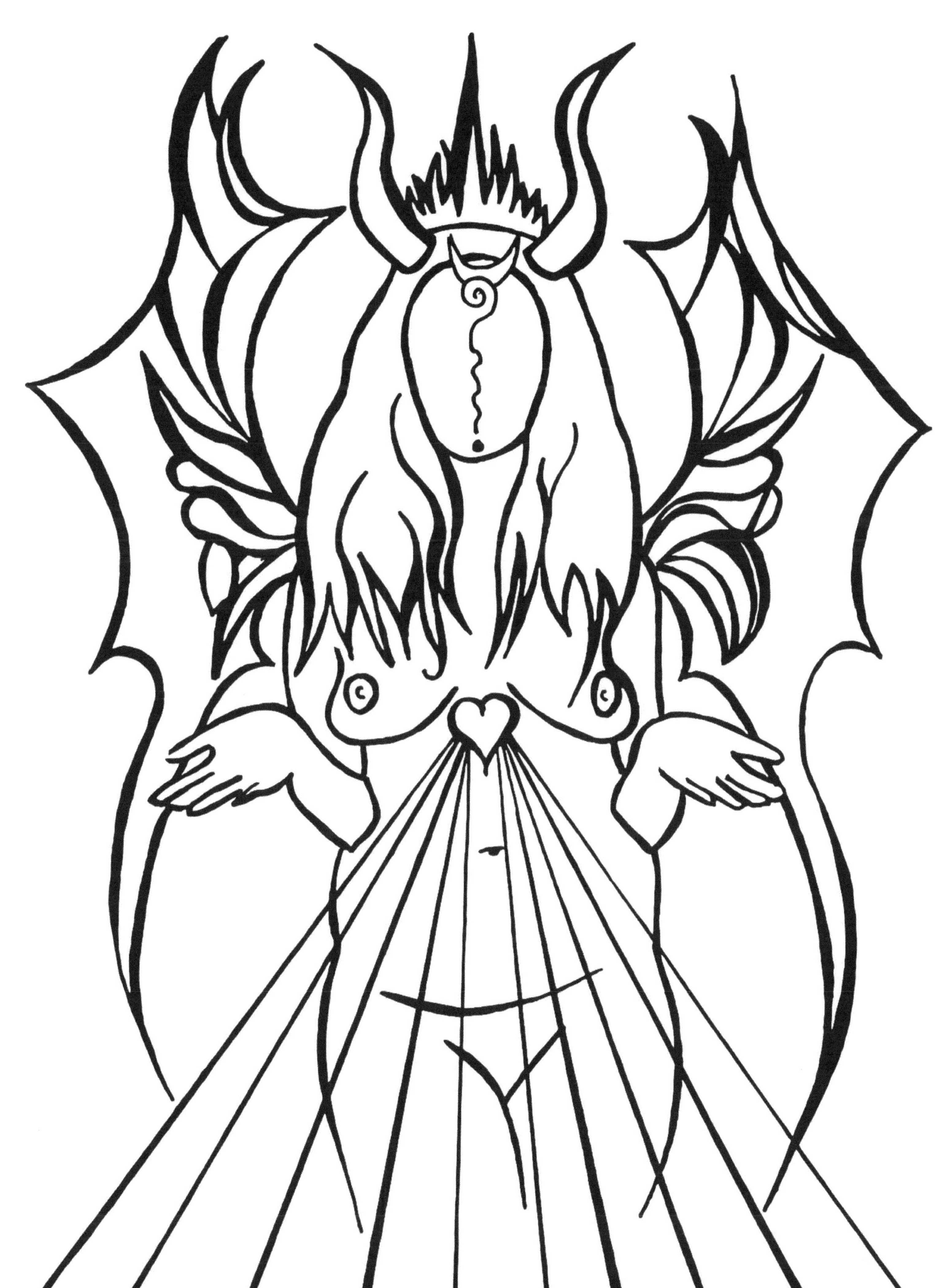

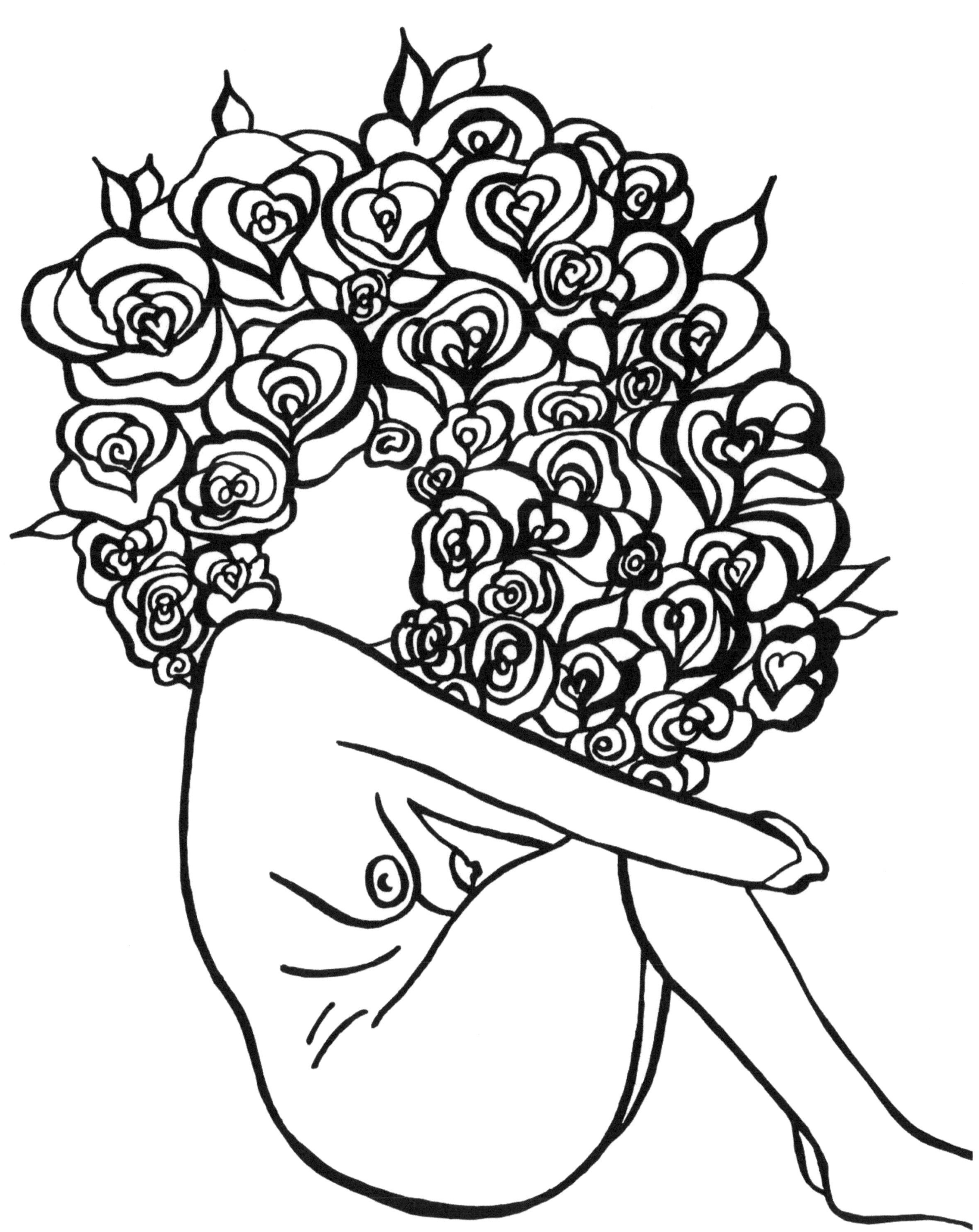

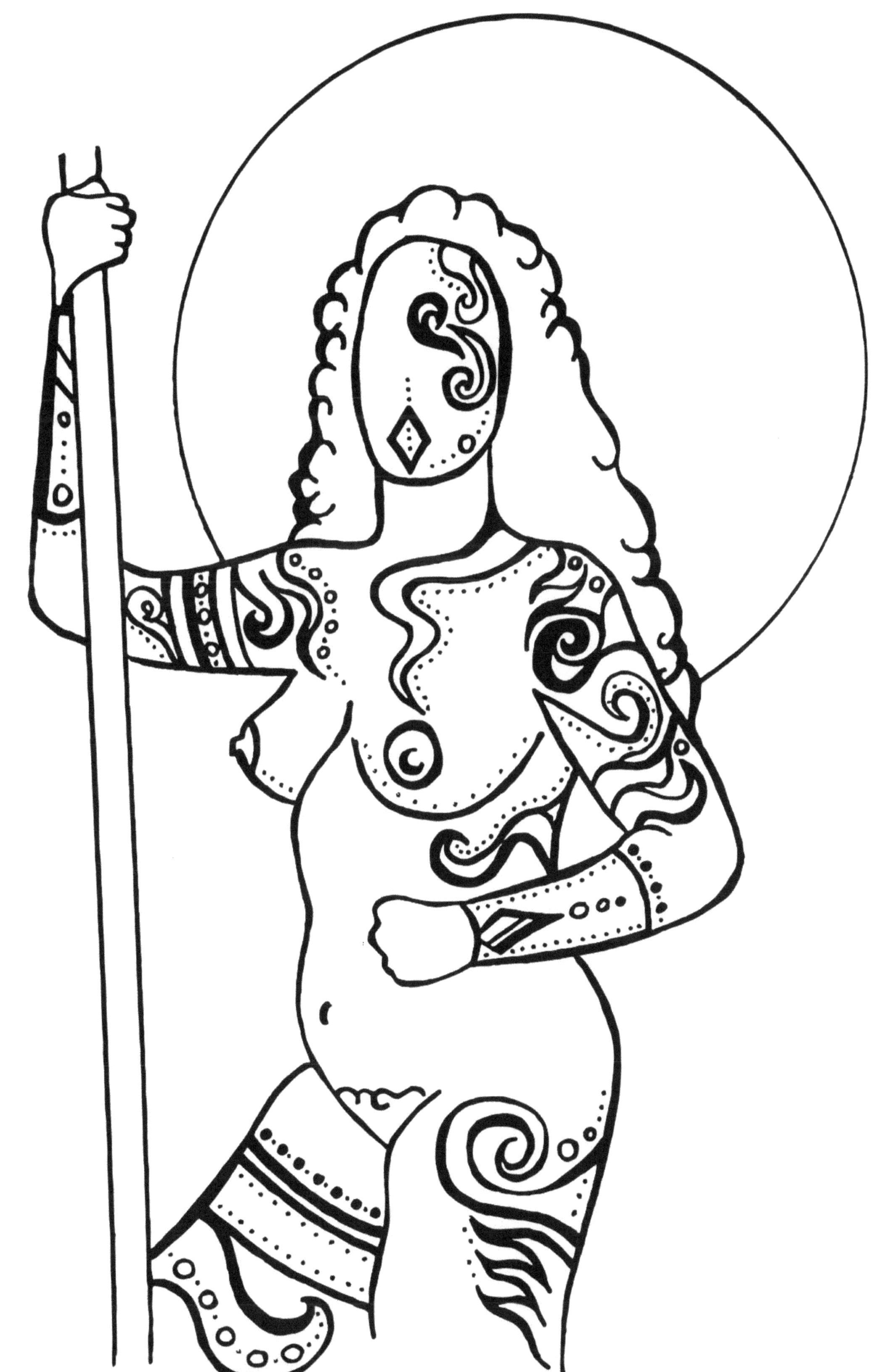

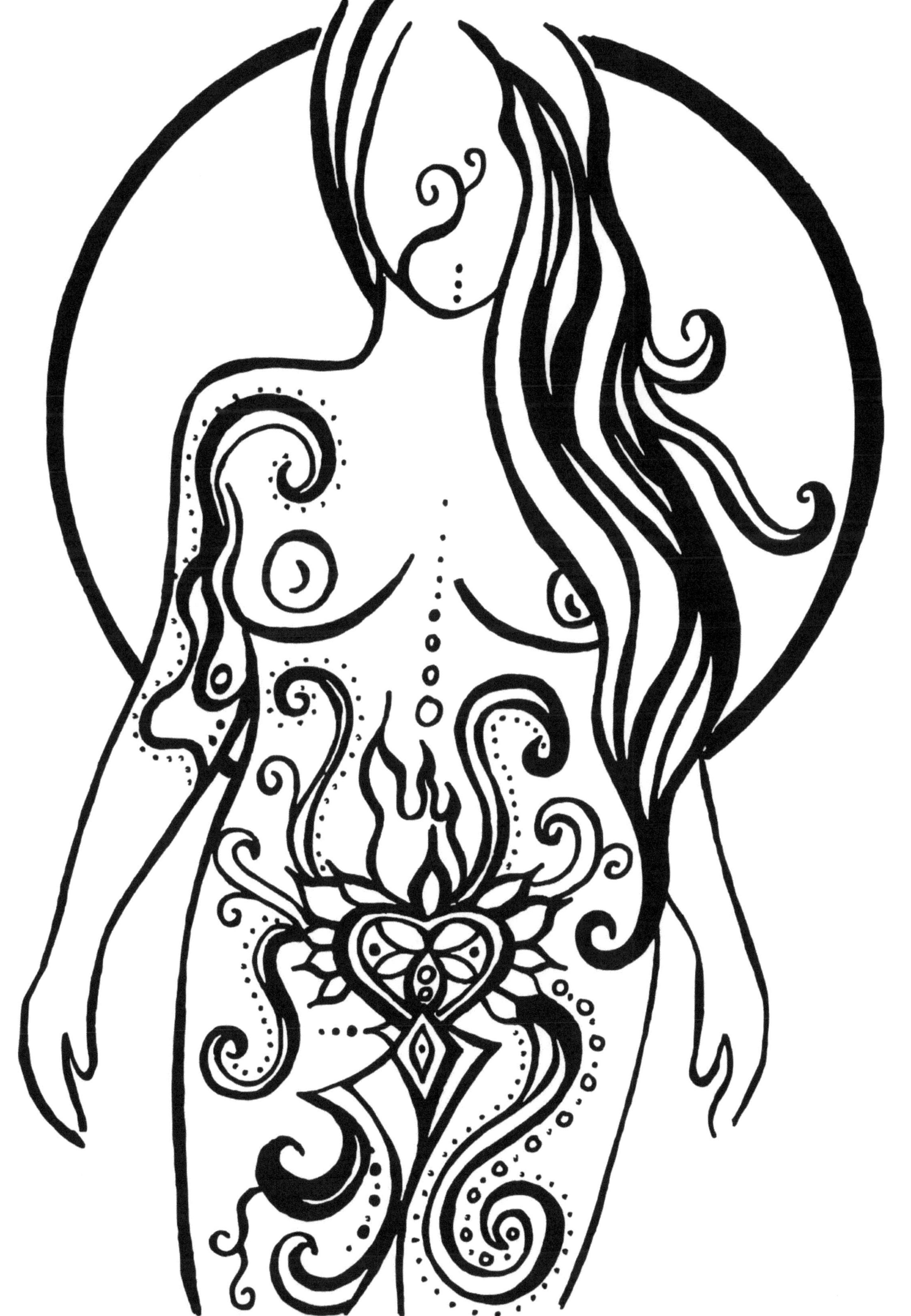

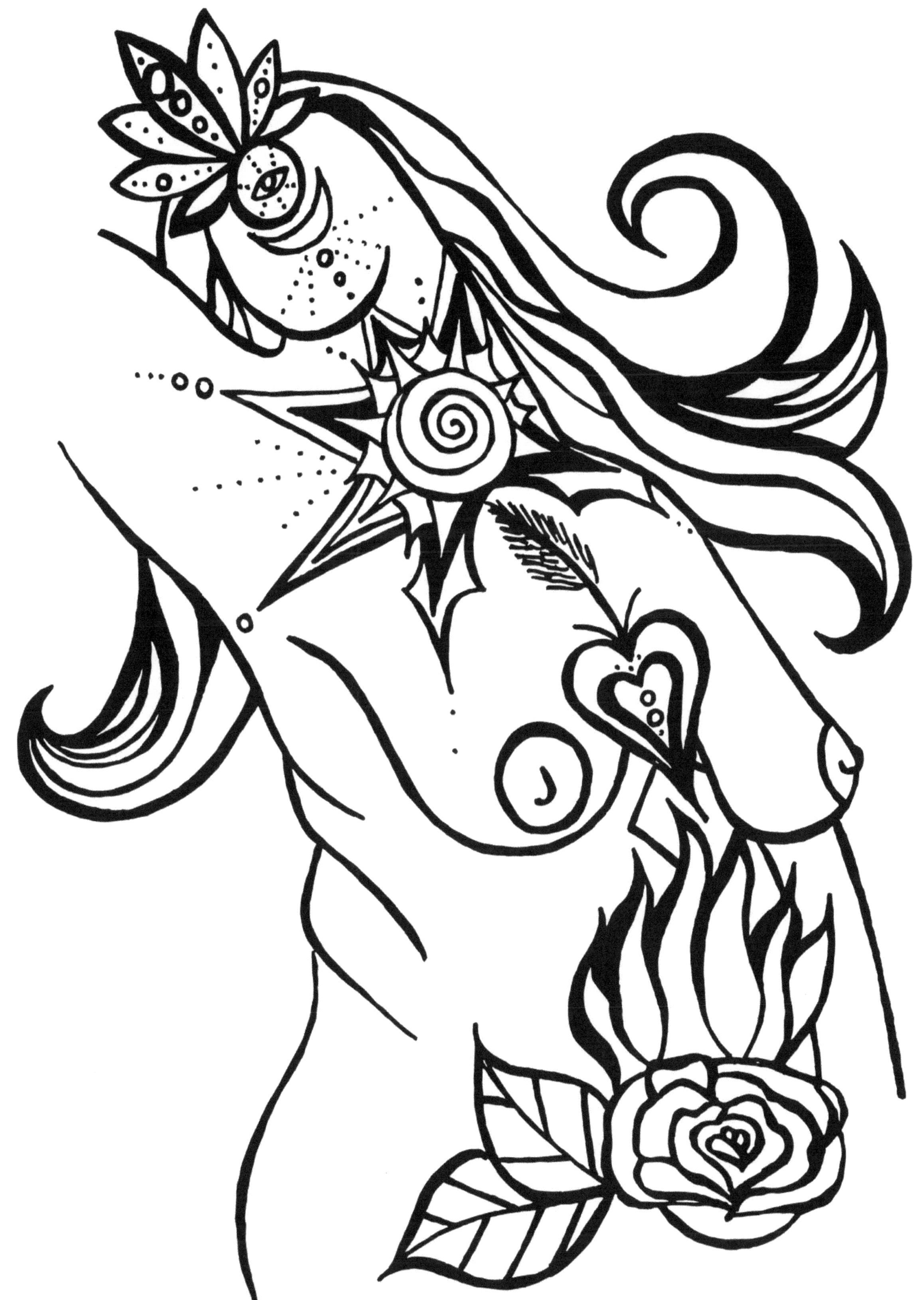

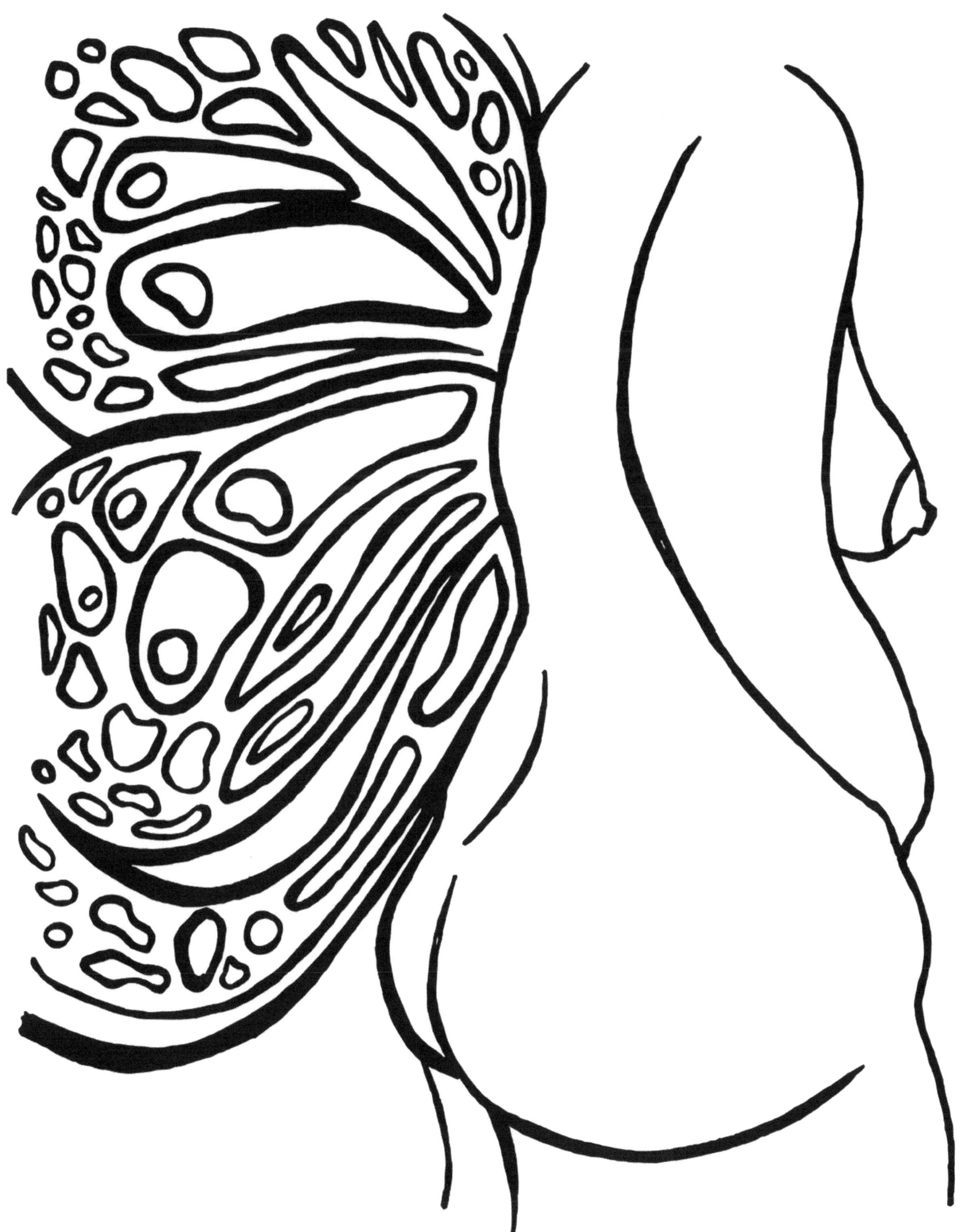

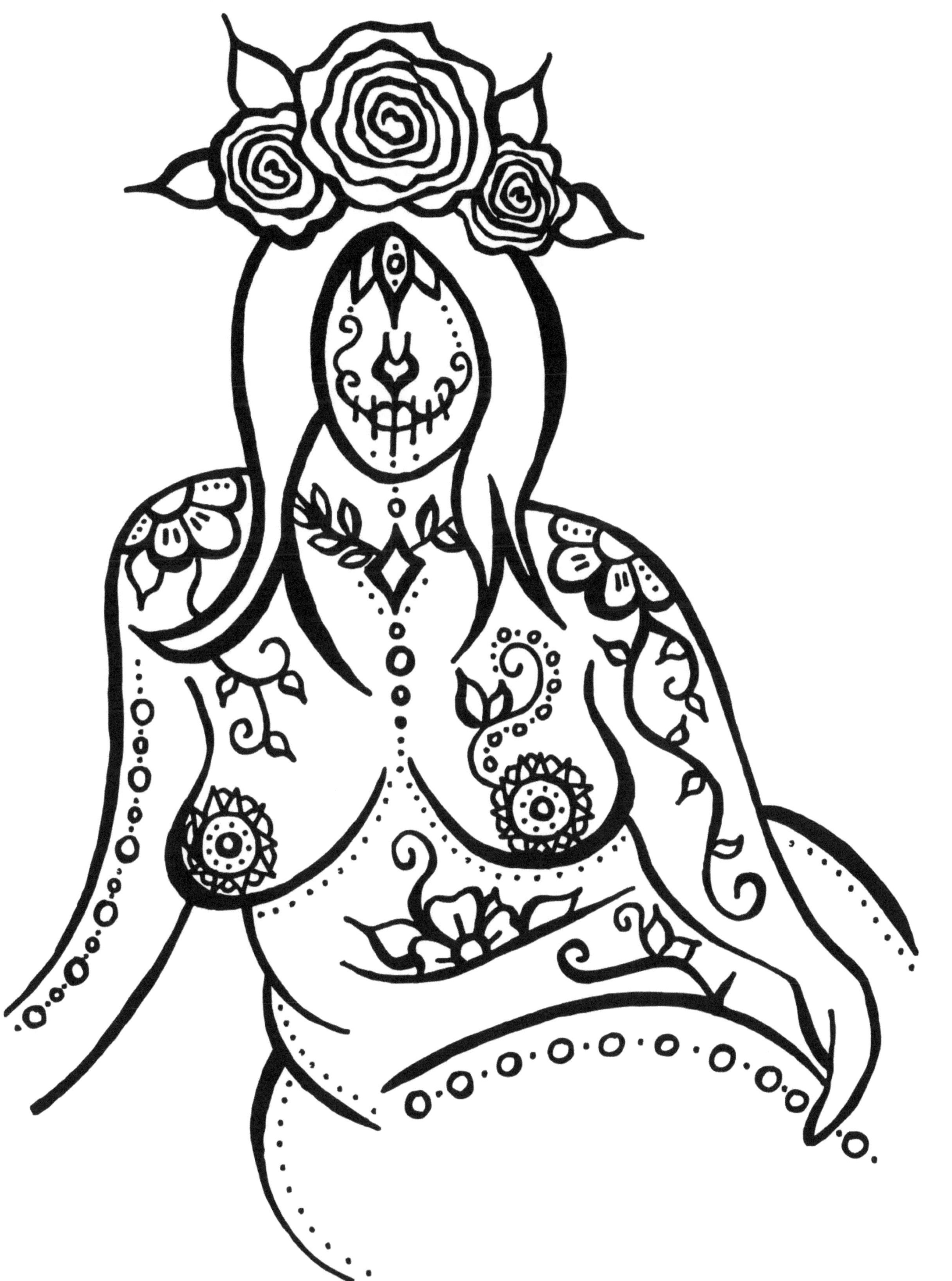

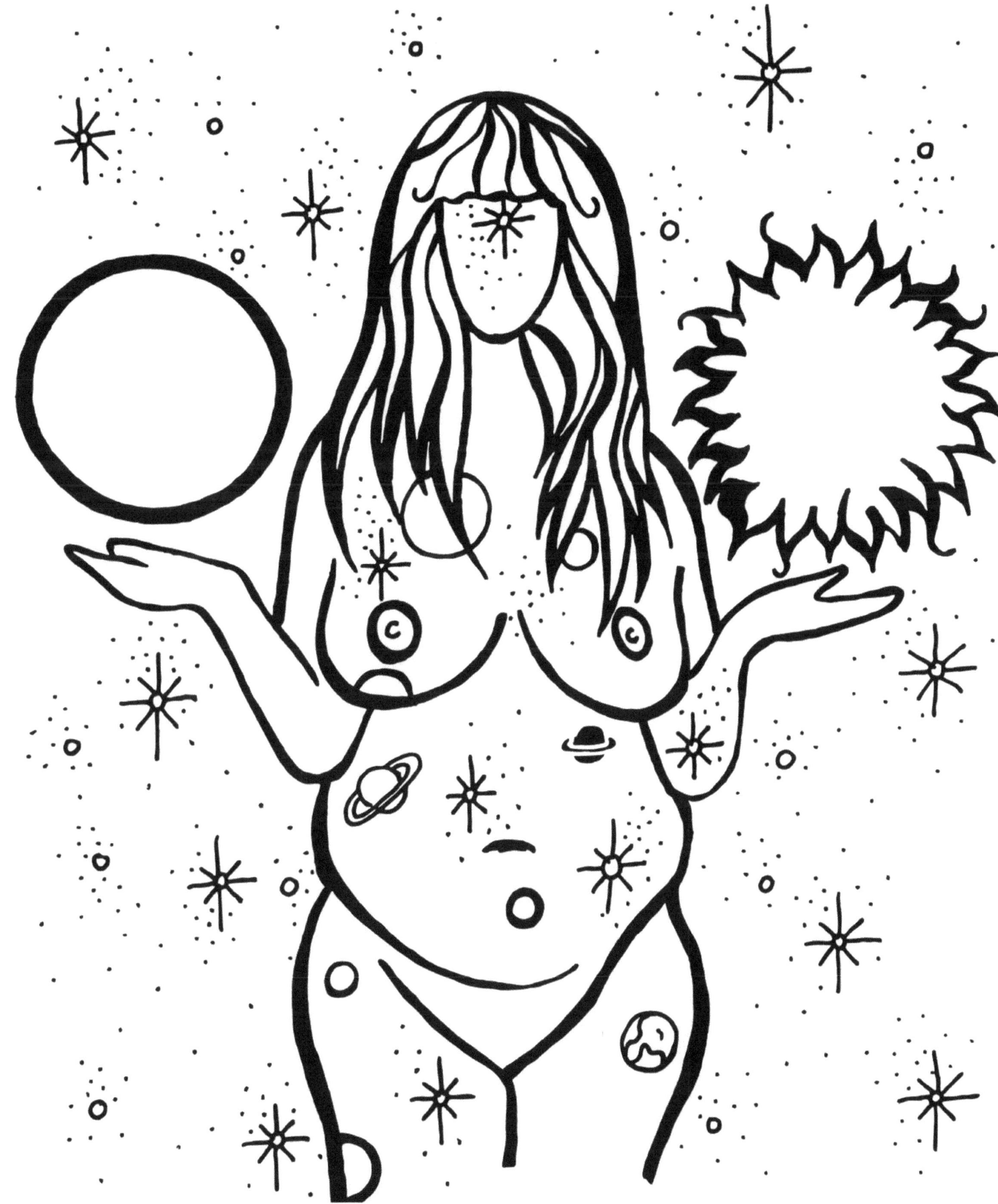

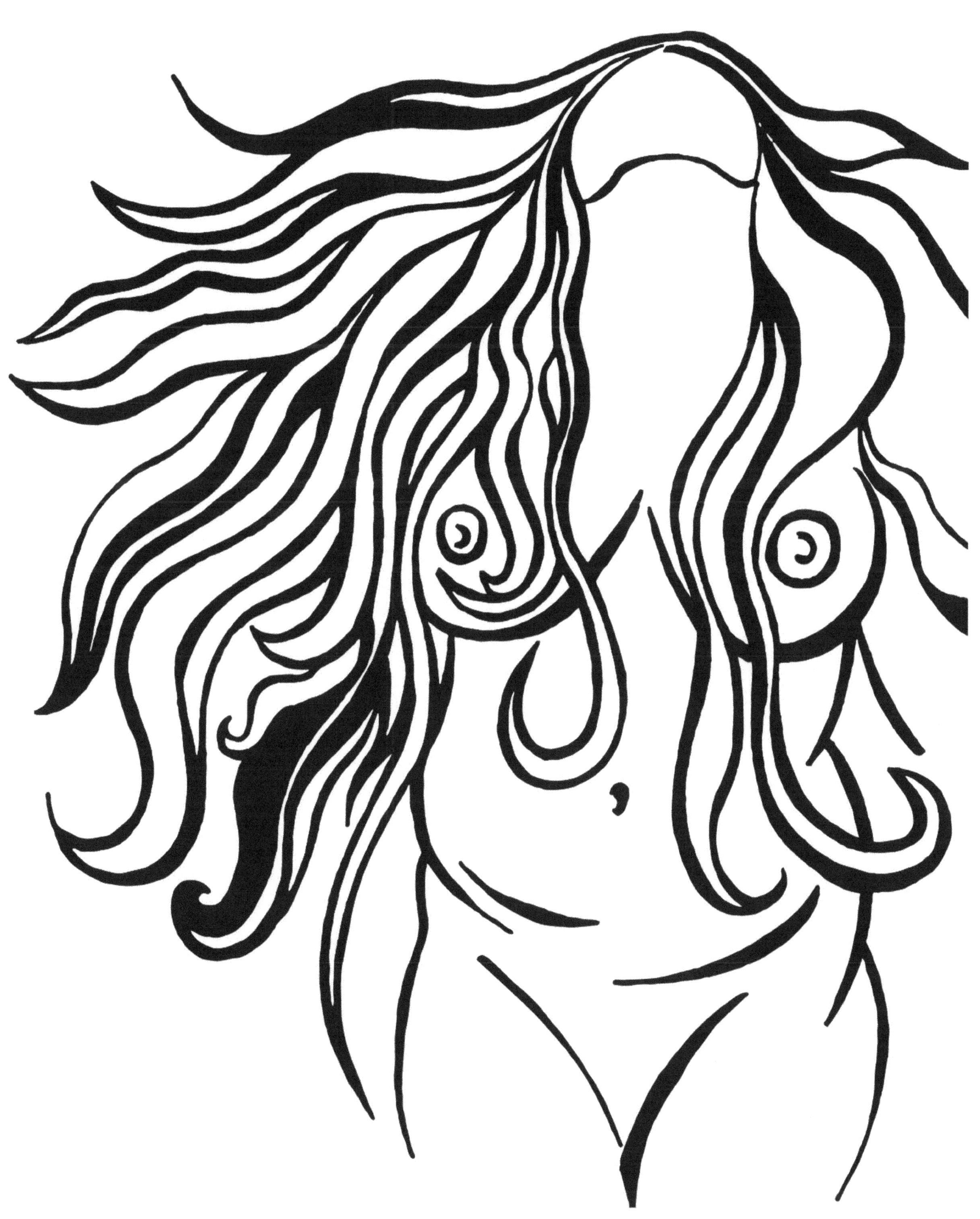

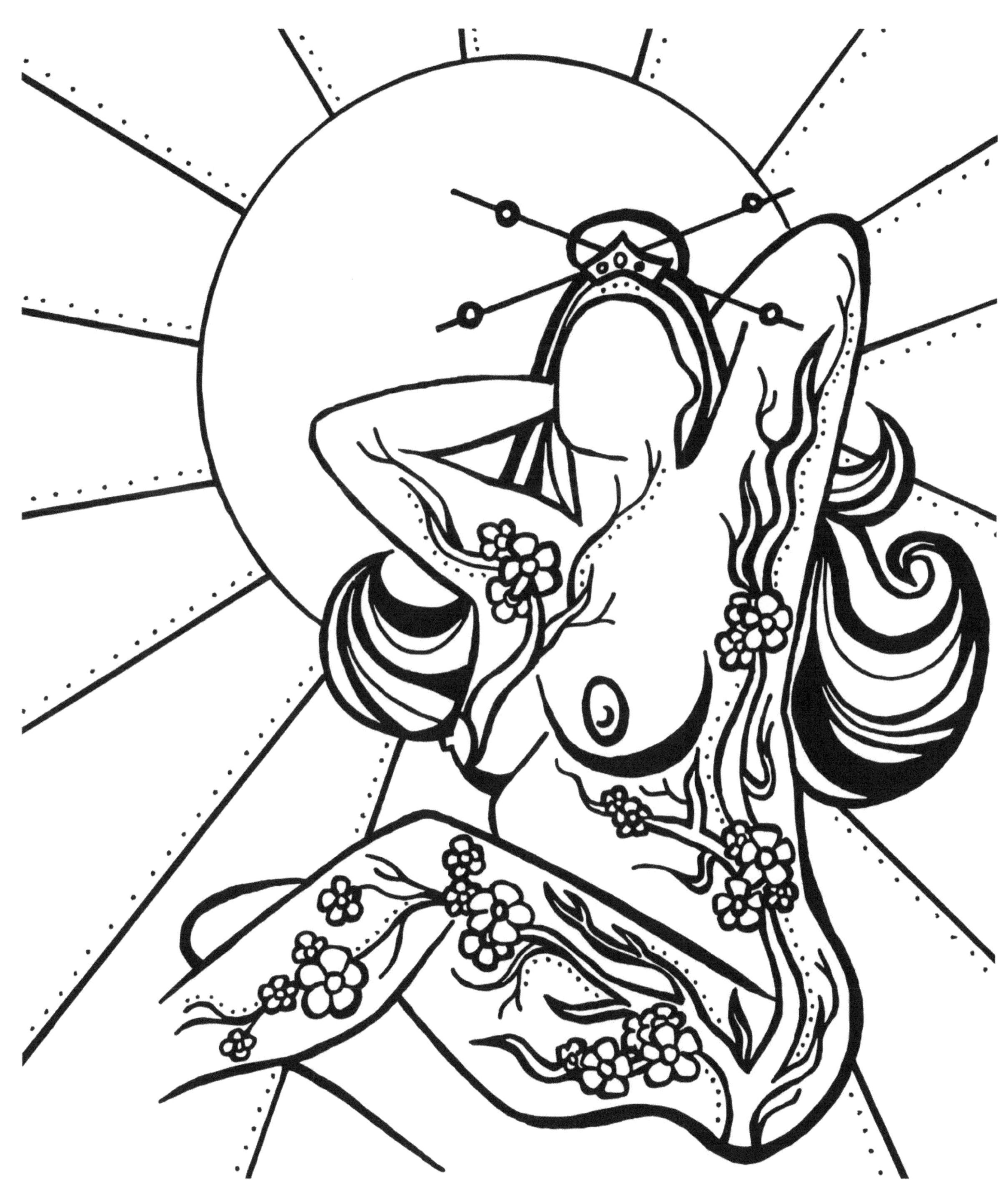

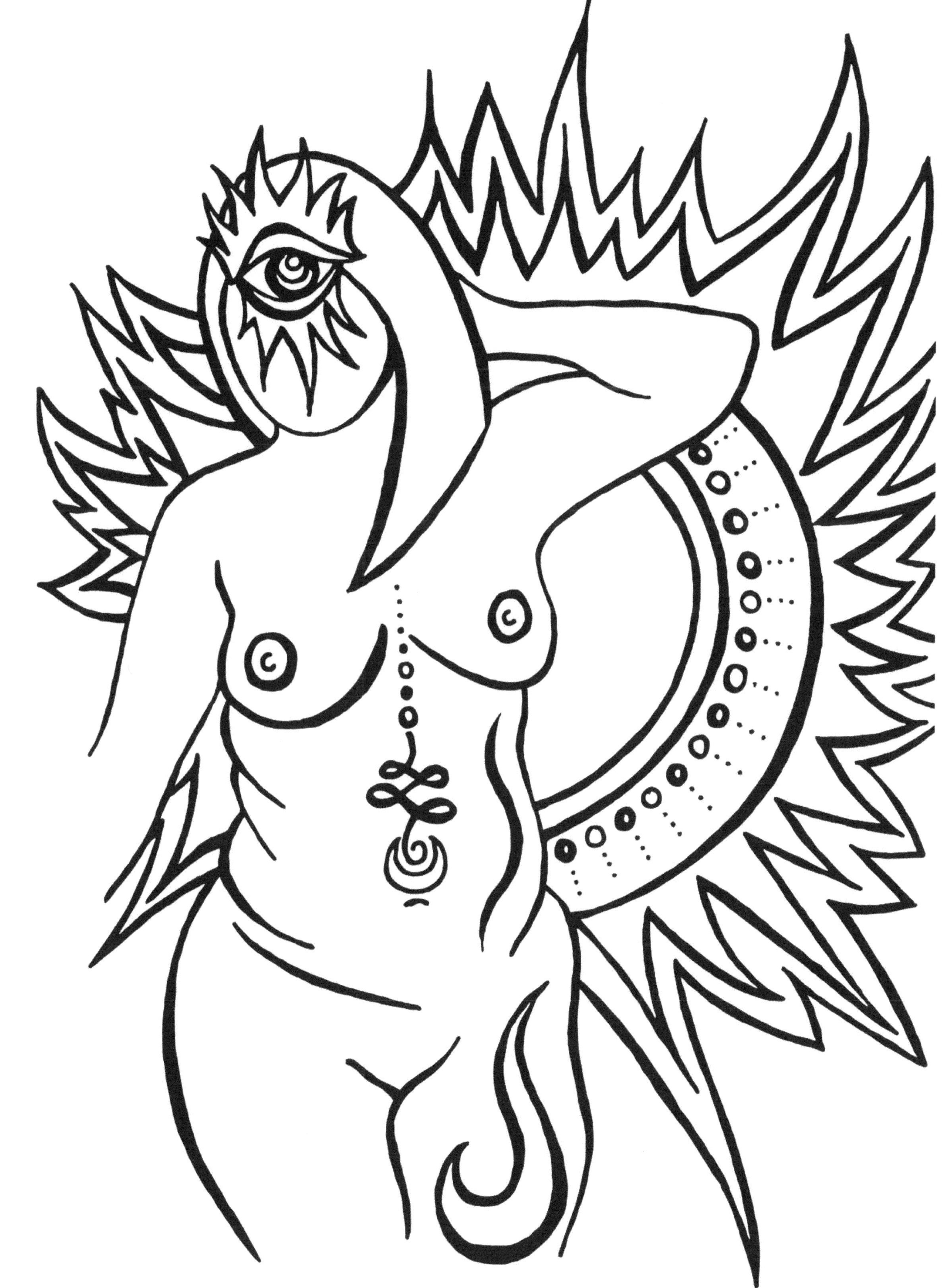

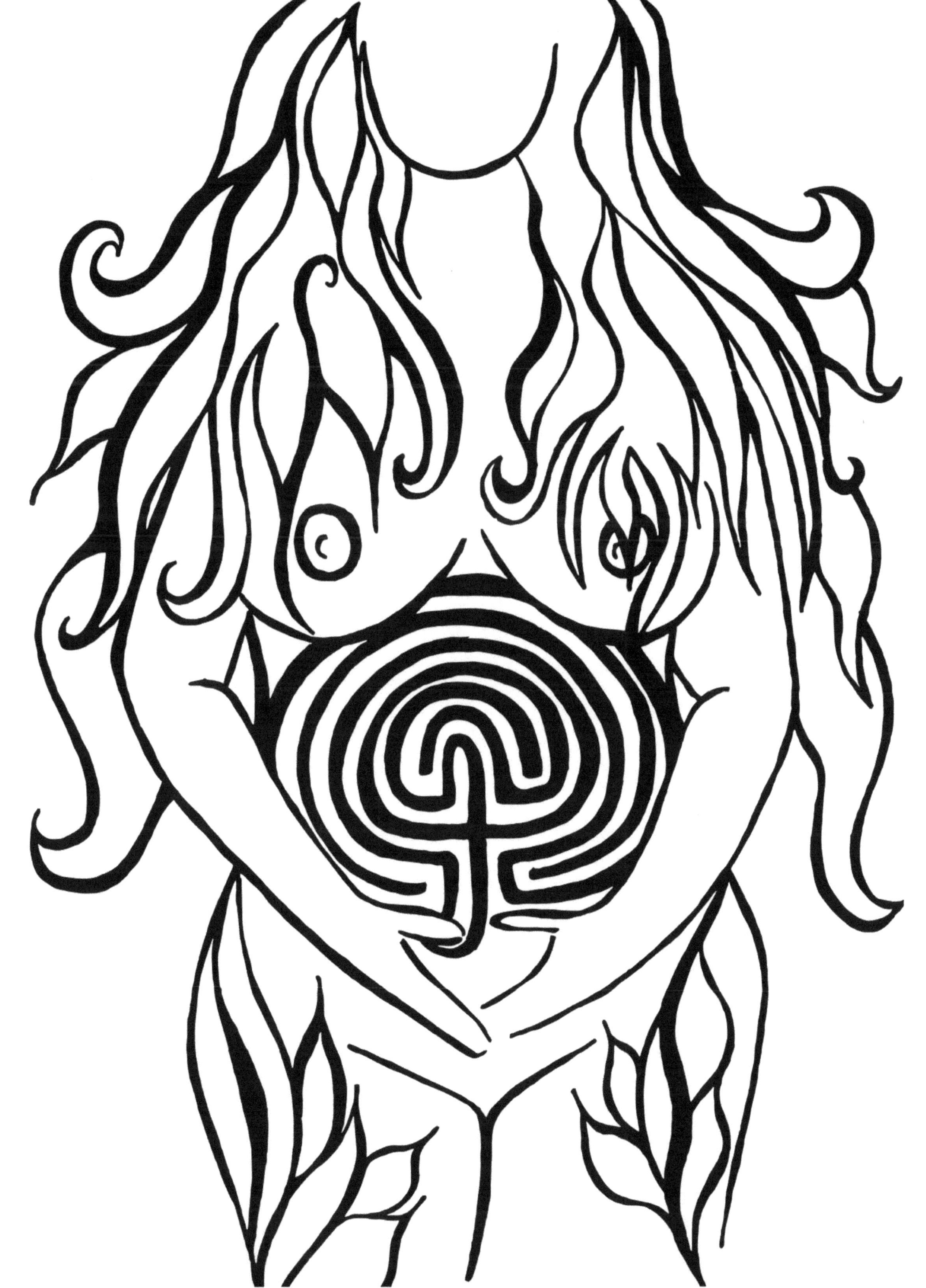

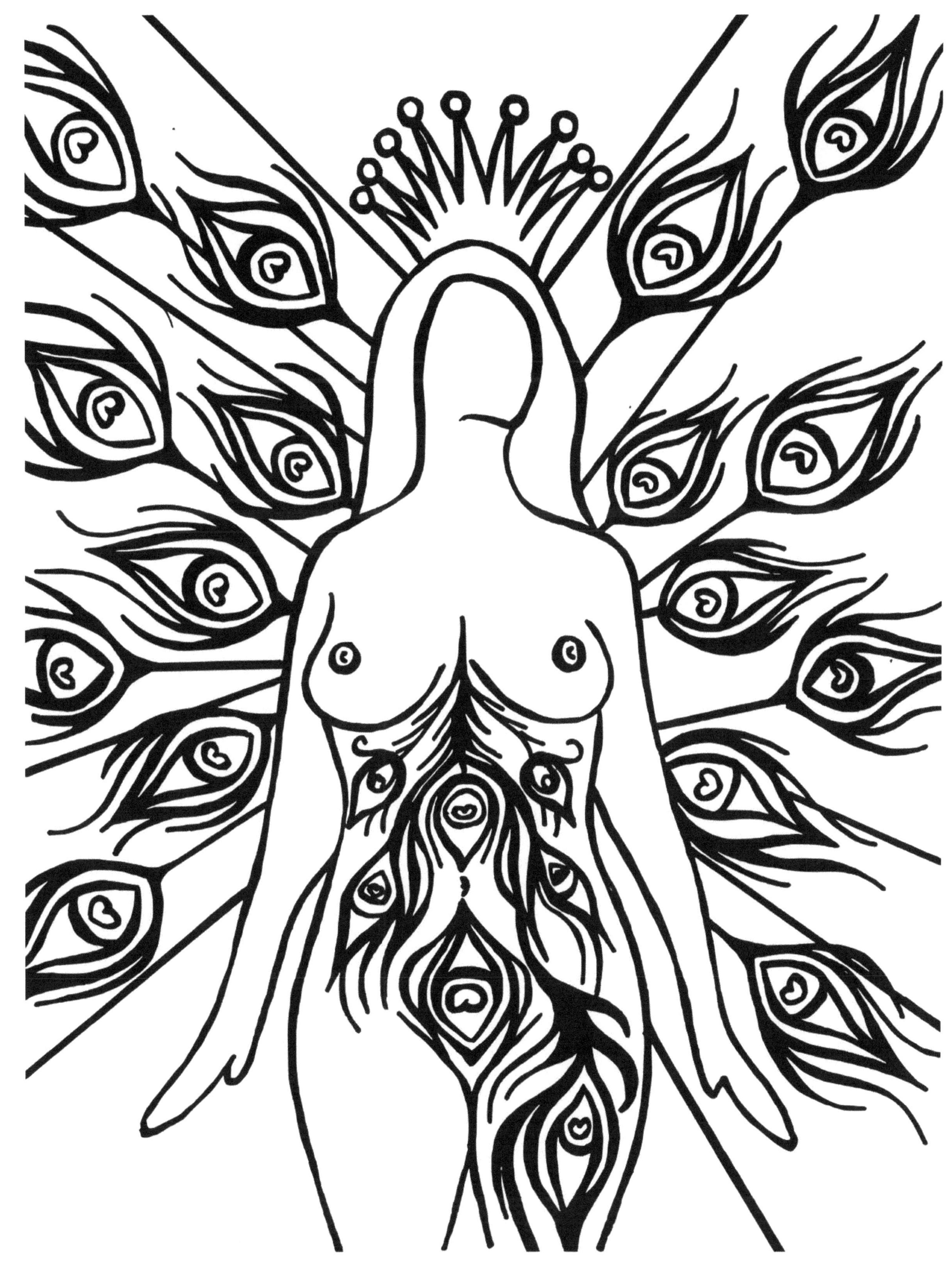

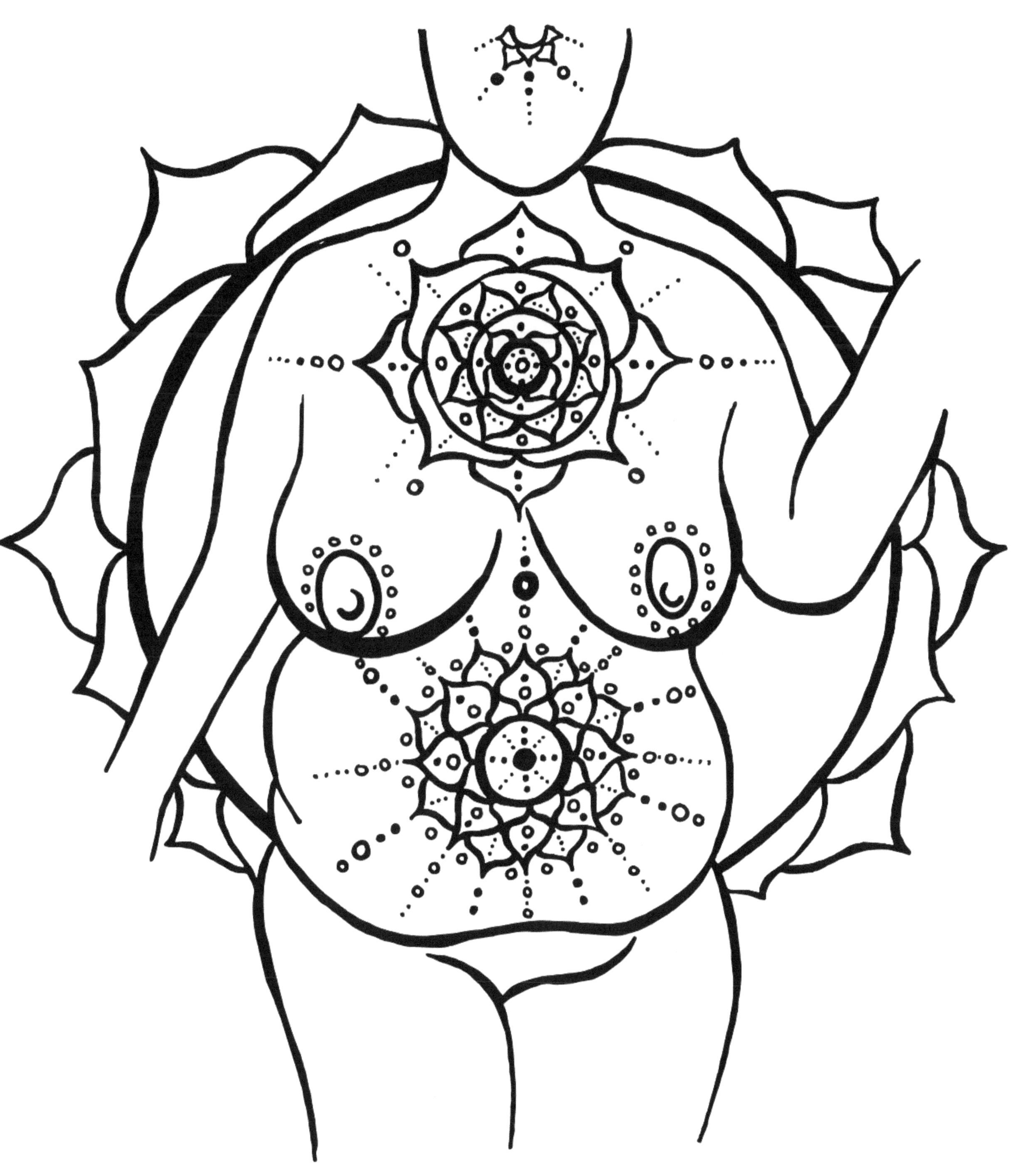

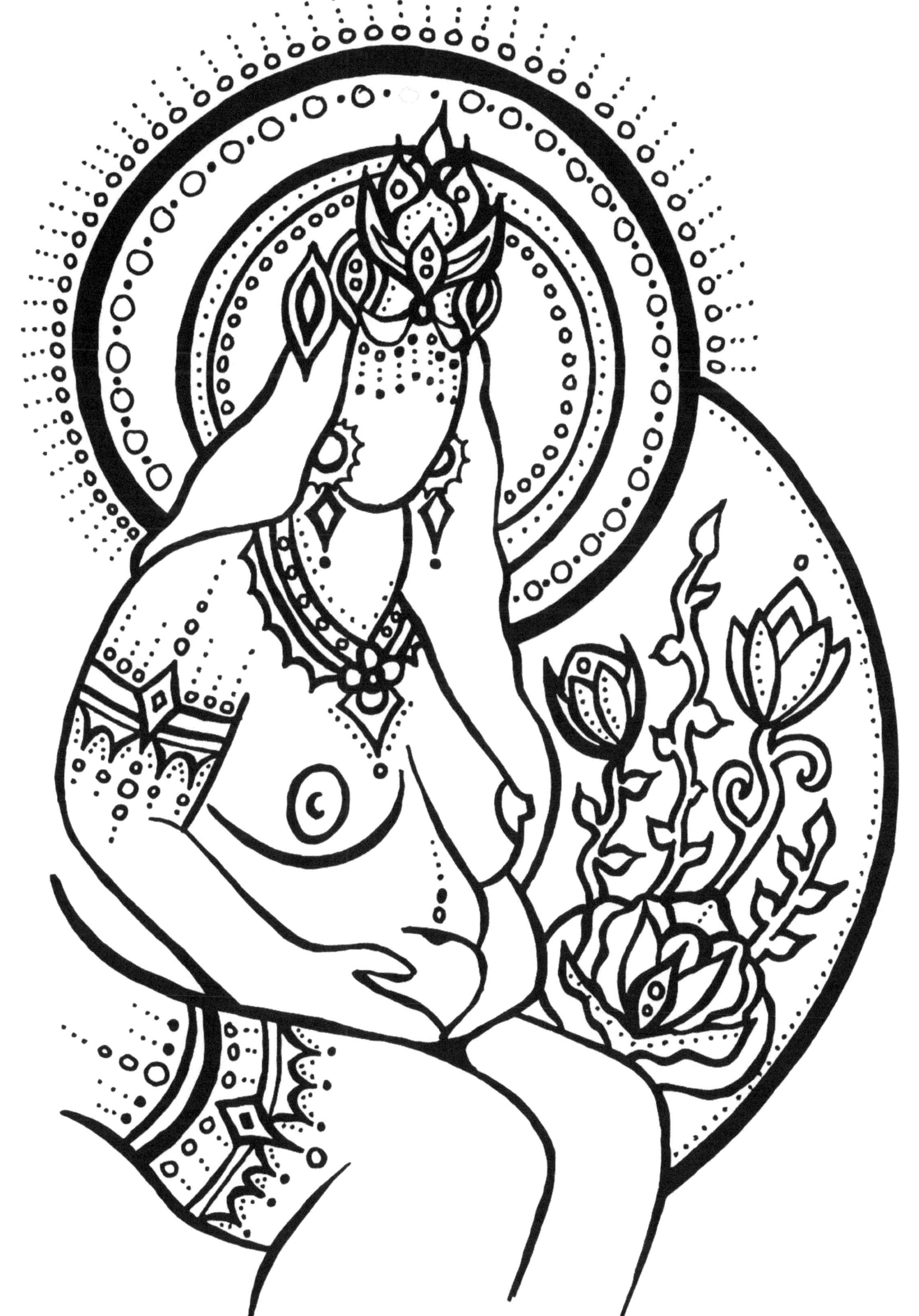

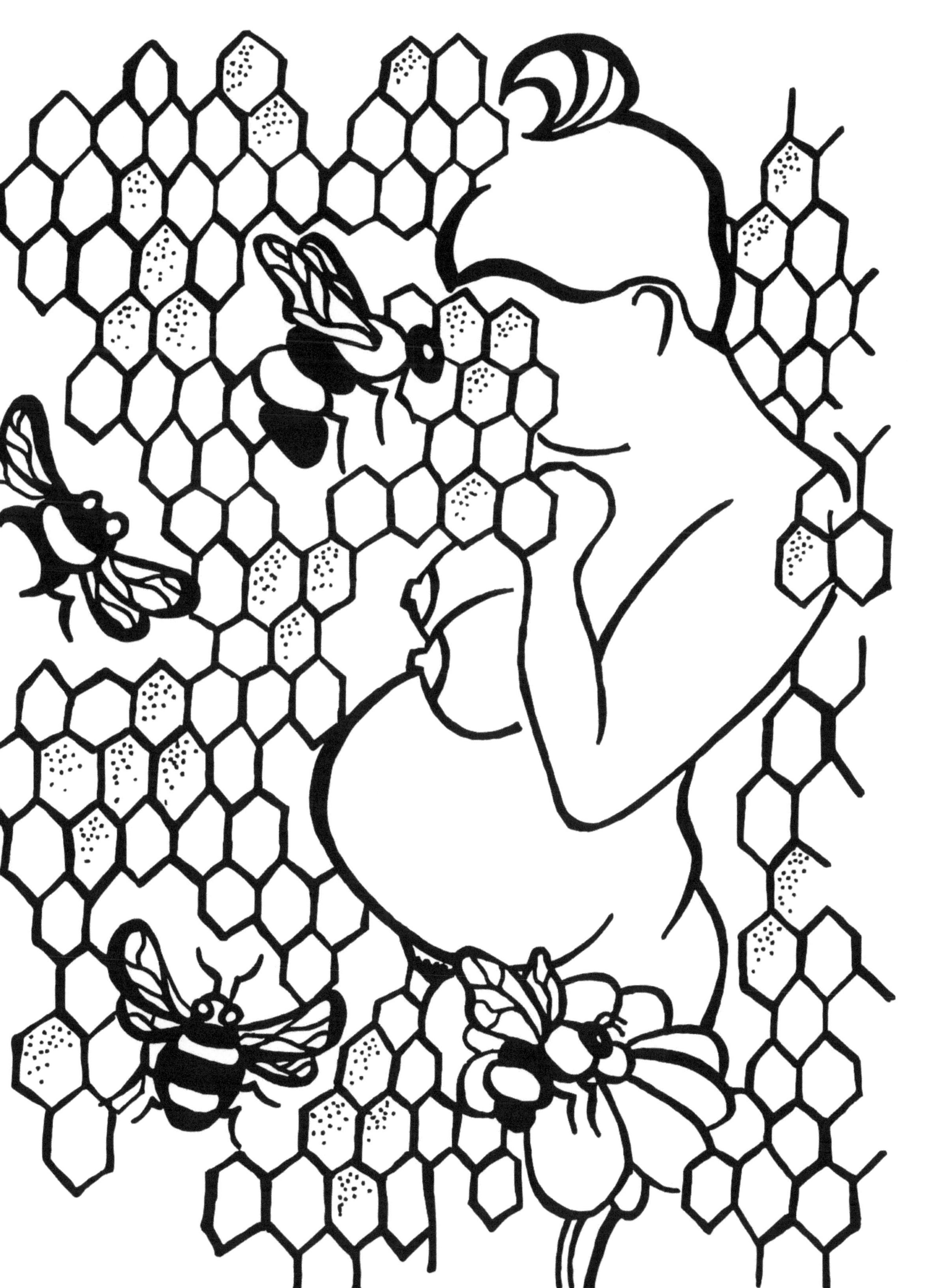

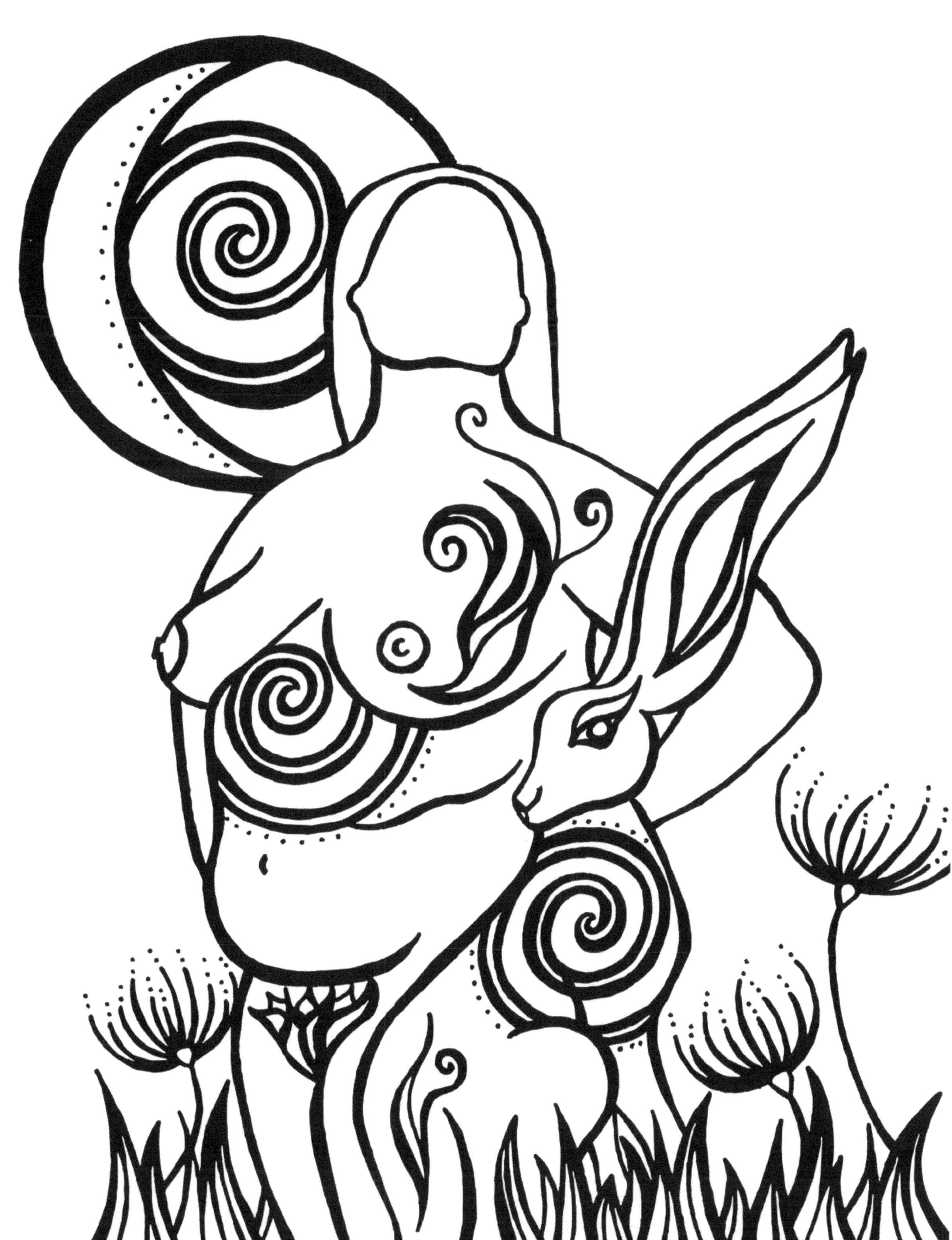

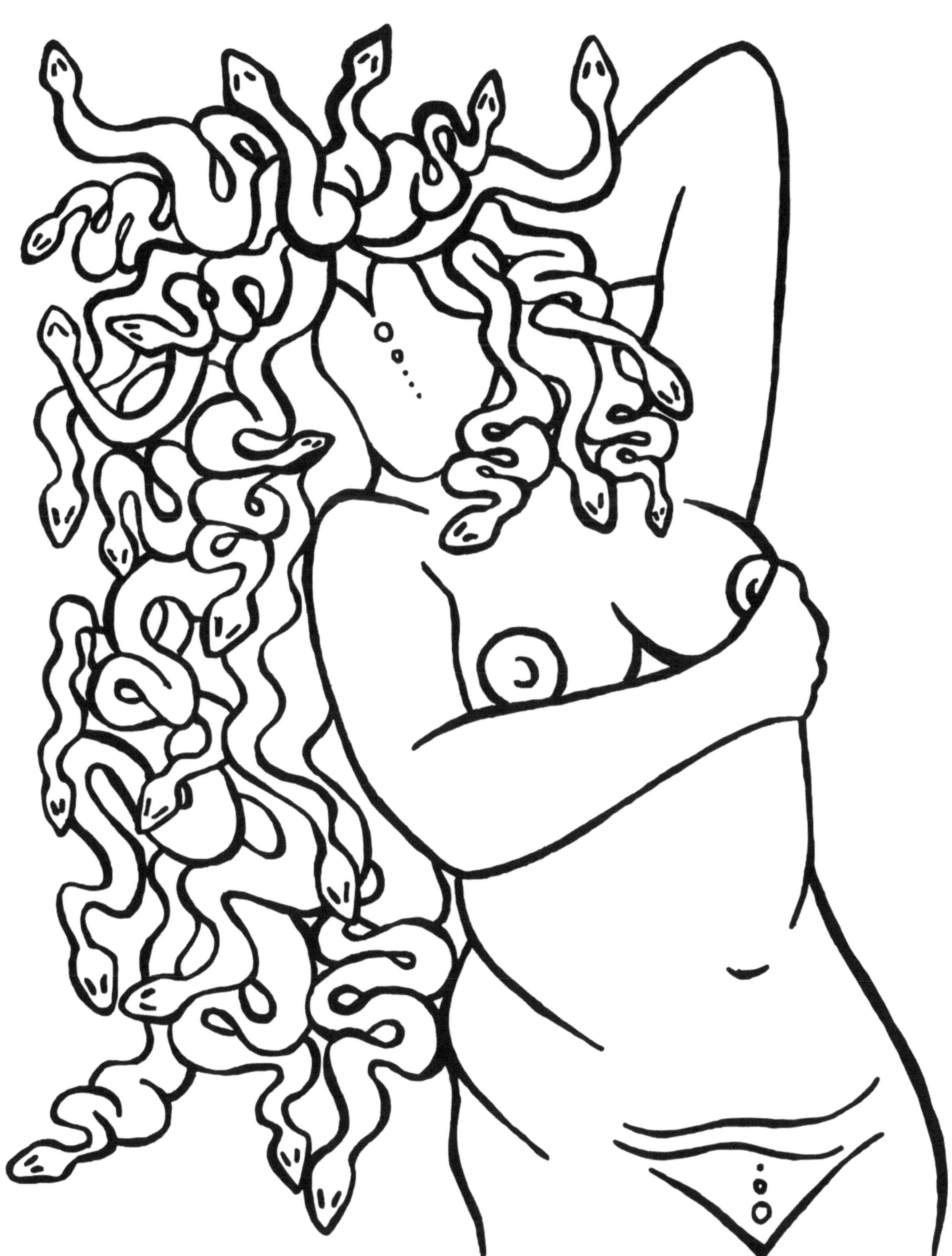

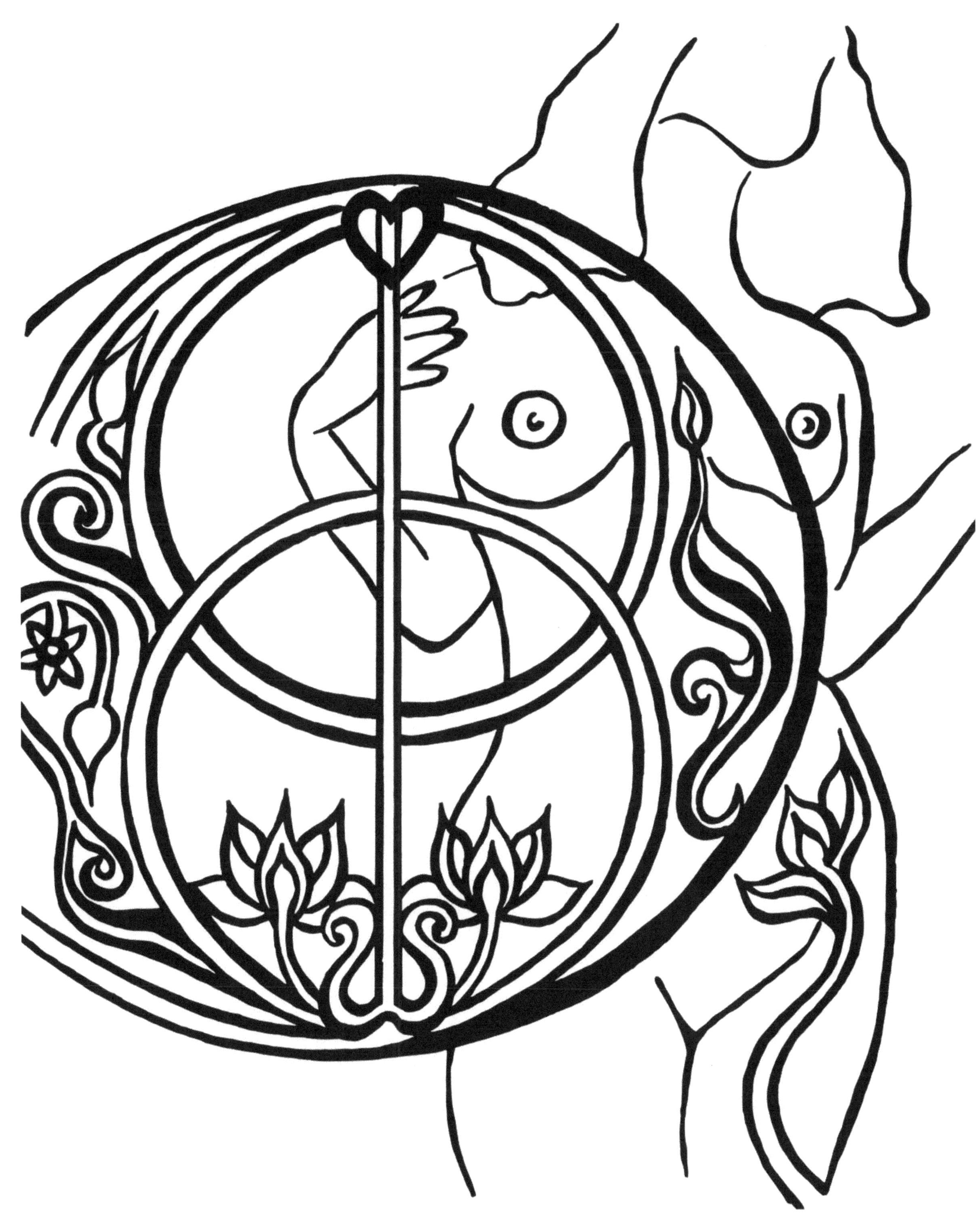

Acknowledgements

This book is for every single Goddess who walks this Earth. May you know your power. May you know your divinity and may you know your gloriousness.

With special thanks to all of my magnificent Goddess muses for sharing your bodies, and all those support me along the way. I see you.

And an extra special thanks to an incredible women who I now call my friend - Trista Hendren. Thanks for standing for all women and for making my dreams come true.

Together, we are the revolution.

STAY TUNED FOR MORE COLOURING BOOKS!